SONGS THAT CHANGED TH

In the late 1960s a youth revival dubbed The Jesus Movement broke out in southern California and around the world. One of the first fruits of that revival was a fresh wave of contemporary music that articulated the faith, passion and vision of a new generation of believers.

Over four decades and thousands of songs later the movement continues. While things like production prowess and songwriting proficiency have certainly improved, at its best moments the Christian music of today echoes with the same heart as those early tunes. Gathered here are thirteen songs that serve as milestones or markers in the growth not only of the genre, but of the body of Christ in this generation.

—John J. Thompson

2 BEAUTIFUL, SCANDALOUS NIGHT

9 BIG HOUSE

16 DIVE

24 FRIENDS

36 GOD OF WONDERS

29 I CAN ONLY IMAGINE

40 INDESCRIBABLE

46 JESUS FREAK

54 SHINE

60 STEP BY STEP

62 TESTIFY TO LOVE

71 THY WORD

76 YOU PUT THIS LOVE IN MY HEART

ISBN 978-1-4234-6923-0

HAL•LEONARD®
CORPORATION
7777 W. BLUEMOUND RD. P.O. BOX 13819 MILWAUKEE, WI 53213

BEAUTIFUL, SCANDALOUS NIGHT

Words and Music by STEVE HINDALONG
and DERRI DAUGHERTY

G C G
to the moun - tain of mer - cy, to the crim -
D G
- son, per - pet - u - al tide.
Kneel
D C G
down on the shore, be thirst - y no more.
Go
D G
un - der and be pu - ri - fied.
Fol - low Christ

G C G
to the ho - ly moun - tain, sin - ner, sor -
- side you will be de - liv - ered, at the foot
D G
- ry and wrecked by the fall. Cleanse
of the cross jus - ti - fied, and your
D C G
your heart and soul in the foun - tain that flows for
spir - it re - stored by the riv - er that pours from
D G
you and for me and for all.
our bless - ed Sav - ior's side.
At the won -

D C G
- der - ful, trag - ic, mys - te - ri - ous tree, on that
D C G
beau - ti - ful, scan - dal - ous night, you and me were a -
D B/D♯ 4fr Em C
toned by His blood and for - ev - er washed white on that
G D 1 G
beau - ti - ful, scan - dal - ous night.

Em7
D/F♯
G
G/B
C(add2)
Ooh, la la la. Ooh,
Em7/B
D/F♯
G
G/B
C(add2)
oh, la la la. On the hill -
2
G
D
At the won - der - ful, trag - ic, mys - te -
C
G
D
- ri - ous tree, on that beau - ti - ful, scan - dal - ous night,

C G D B/D♯
4fr
you and me were a - toned by His blood and for -
Em C G D
ev - er washed white on that beau - ti - ful, scan - dal - ous night.
G D
Oh, it was a beau - ti - ful, scan - dal - ous night.
G Em7 D/F♯ G G/B
Oh, la la la la

C(add2)
Em7
D/F♯
la.
Oh,
G
G/B
1
C(add2)
la
la
la,
2
C(add2)
la.
Ooh,
la
la
la.
La
la
Repeat ad lib. and Fade
Optional Ending
la,
la
la
la.

BIG HOUSE

Words and Music by MARK STUART,
BARRY BLAIR, WILL McGINNISS
and BOB HERDMAN

A
F♯m
D
E
D
I don't know where you eat your meals or where you talk on the phone.
I don't know if you live with friends in whom you can con - fide.
A
F♯m
D
I don't know if you got a cook, a but - ler or a maid.
I don't know if you got a fam - 'ly, say, a mom or dad.
A
F♯m
1
D
E
D
I don't know if you got a yard with a ham - mock in the shade.
I don't know if you feel love at all, but I
A
E
2
D
E
D
bet you wish you had.

A E D A/C♯ Bm Esus A E
Come and go with me to my Fa-ther's house. Come and go with me
D A/C♯ Bm E A E
to my Fa-ther's house. It's a big, big house with lots and lots of
A E A
room; a big, big ta - ble with lots and lots of food; a big, big
E A To Coda E
yard where we can play foot - ball; a big, big house. It's my Fa-ther's

A
E
A
house.
E
A
F♯m
D
All I know is a big ol' house _ with rooms for ev - 'ry - one. _
A
F♯m
D
E
D
A
F♯m
All I know is lots of land _ where we can play and run.
All I know is you need love, _ and
D.S. al Coda
D
A
F♯m
D
E
D
I've got a fam - i - ly. _____
All I know is you're all a - lone, _ so why not come with me?

CODA
E
A
E
house. It's my Fa-ther's house. A big, big house with lots and lots of
A
E
A
room; a big, big ta - ble with lots and lots of food; a big, big
E
A
E
yard where we can play foot - ball; a big, big house. It's my Fa-ther's
A
house. My Fa-ther's house.
(Vocal 1st time only)

N.C.
Come and go with me _ to my Fa-ther's house. _
Come and go with me _ to my Fa - ther's house. It's a big, big
house with lots and lots _ of room; _ a big, big ta - ble with lots and lots _ of
food; a big, big yard where we can play _ foot - ball; a big, big

E
A
E
house. It's my Fa-ther's house. A big, big house with lots and lots of
A
E
room; a big, big ta - ble with lots and lots of
A
E
A
food; a big, big yard where we can play foot - ball; a big, big
E
N.C.
A
house. It's my Fa-ther's house.

DIVE

Words and Music by
STEVEN CURTIS CHAPMAN

C♭maj7
D♭
they've carved their way to where the wild and rush - ing riv - er can be found.
It can bring the dead to life and it can fill an emp - ty soul
C♭maj7
D♭
And like the rain I have been car - ried here to where the riv - er flows,
and give our heart the on - ly thing worth liv - ing and worth dy -
E♭
A♭sus2
G♭
C♭maj7
yeah.
- ing for, yeah.
D♭
My heart is rac - ing and my knees are weak as I walk to the edge.
But we will nev - er know the awe - some pow - er of the grace of God

C♭maj7
D♭
I know there is no turn-ing back a-once my feet have left the ledge.
un-til we let our-selves get swept a-way in-to this ho-ly flood.
C♭maj7
D♭
And in the rush, I hear a voice that's tell-ing me it's time to take
So, if you take my hand, we'll close our eyes and count to three and take
C♭maj7
B♭sus
E♭5
B♭5
the leap of faith, so here I go.
the leap of faith. Come on, let's go.
I'm div-ing in; I'm go-ing deep,
6fr
Cm7
A♭5
B♭5
E♭5
B♭5
3fr
4fr
6fr
in o-ver my head. I wan-na be caught in the rush, lost in the flow.

Cm7
A♭5
B♭5
E♭5
B♭5
In o-ver my head I wan-na go. The riv-er's deep; the riv-er's wide;
Cm7
A♭5
B♭5
C♭(add2)
D♭(add2)
the riv-er's wa - ter is a-live, so sink or swim, I'm div-ing in.
1
E♭
A♭sus2
E♭
A♭sus2

2
E♭
3fr
B♭
A♭
4fr
I'm div - ing in.
Oh,
I'm div - ing in,
yeah, hah.
I'm div - ing in,
yeah,
here I go.

A♭ G♭ E♭
A♭ G♭ C♭maj7 A♭ G♭ E♭
A♭ G♭ C♭maj7
E♭5 B♭5
Come on, let's go. I'm div - ing in; I'm go - ing deep,

Cm7 A♭5 B♭5 E♭5 B♭5
3fr 4fr 6fr
in o - ver my head. I wan - na be caught in the rush, lost in the flow,
Cm7 A♭5 B♭5 E♭5 B♭5
3fr 4fr 6fr
in o - ver my head I wan - na go. The riv - er's deep; the riv - er's wide;
Cm7 A♭5 B♭5 C♭(add2) D♭(add2)
3fr 4fr 4fr
the riv - er's wa - ter is a - live, so sink or swim, I'm div - ing in.
C♭(add2) B♭sus C♭(add2) D♭(add2)
4fr 4fr
So sink or swim, I'm div - ing in. So sink or swim,

Eb5 Bb5 Cm7 Ab5 Bb5
I'm div - ing in. Whoa,
Eb5 Bb5 Cm7 Ab5 Bb5
whoa. I'm div - ing in.
Eb5 Bb5 Cm7 Ab5 Bb5
Whoa,
(I'm div - ing in; I'm go - ing deep.)
Eb5 Bb5 Cm7 Ab5 Bb5 Eb5
whoa. I'm div - ing in.
(In o-ver my head I wan-na be,) (I'm div-ing in.)

FRIENDS

Words and Music by MICHAEL W. SMITH
and DEBORAH D. SMITH

G
Bm/F♯
Em(add2)
Em
Can't be - lieve the hopes He's grant - ed means a
we will pray the joy you'll live in
Am
Em/G
D/F♯
chap - ter in your life is through.
is the strength that now you show.
But we'll keep you close
Dm/F
Esus
E
Am(add2)
Am
as al - ways; it won't e - ven seem you've gone.
Cm
3fr
G
Bm/F♯
Em(add2)
Em
'Cause our hearts, in big and small ways, will

Am D/F♯ C(add2)/G D/G G C/D D
keep the love_ that keeps_ us strong. And_
G D/F♯ C/E Dsus D
friends are friends_ for - ev - er if the Lord's the Lord_ of them._ And a
mf
G D/F♯ C/E Dsus D
friend will not_ say "nev - er," 'cause the wel - come will_ not end._ Though it's
Bsus B Em C(add2)
hard to let_ you go,_ in the Fa - ther's hands_ we know_ that a

Am7
D7sus
1
G
D/F♯
life-time's not too long to live as friends.
dim.
mp
C/E
D7sus
2
G
E♭
3fr
D♭/E♭
A♭
E♭/G
And friends are friends for-ev - er if the
f
D♭/F
E♭7sus
6fr
E♭7
A♭
E♭/G
Lord's the Lord of them. And a friend will not say "nev - er," 'cause the
D♭/F
E♭7sus
6fr
E♭7
Csus
C
wel - come will not end. Though it's hard to let you go, in the

Fm
D♭
B♭m7
Fa - ther's hands we know that a life - time's not too long
dim.
mf
E♭7sus
C7/E
Fm(add2)
Fm
to live as friends. No, a
dim.
B♭m7
B♭m7(add4)
4fr
E♭7sus
life - time's not too long to live as friends.
mp
molto rit.
A♭
4fr
E♭/G
3fr
D♭/F
E♭sus
6fr
E♭
3fr
A♭
4fr
a tempo
rit.

I CAN ONLY IMAGINE

Words and Music by
BART MILLARD

Emaj9
Amaj9
mag - ine.
Asus2
Sur - round - ed by Your glo - ry, what
mf
B(add4)
E(add2)
will my heart feel? Will I dance for You, Je - sus, or in
E
Emaj7
Asus2
awe of You be still? Will I stand in Your pres - ence or to my

B(add4)
E(add2)
knees will I fall? Will I sing hal - le - lu - jah? Will I be
E
Emaj7
Asus2
To Coda
a - ble to speak at all? I can on - ly i - mag - ine,
B(add4)
Emaj7
I can on - ly i - mag - ine. I can on - ly i -
Amaj9
mag - ine when that day comes and I find my - self stand - ing in

B7sus
Emaj7
the Son. I can on - ly i - mag - ine when all I will do is for-ev -
Amaj9
B7sus
Emaj7
- er, for-ev - er wor - ship You. I can on - ly i - mag - ine,
Amaj9
B7sus
D.S. al Coda
I can on - ly i - mag - ine. Sur-
CODA
B(add4)
E
I can on - ly i - mag - ine.

Asus2
Sur-round - ed by Your glo - ry, what
f
Bsus
Emaj7
E
will my heart feel? Will I dance for You, Je - sus, or in
Emaj7
E
Asus2
awe of You be still? Will I stand in Your pres - ence or to my
Bsus
Emaj7
E
knees will I fall? Will I sing hal - le - lu - jah? Will I be

Emaj7 E Asus2
a - ble to speak at all? I can on - ly i - mag - ine, yeah,
Bsus Emaj7 E Emaj7 E
I can on-ly i-mag - ine. I can on-ly i-mag -
Asus2 Bsus
- ine, yeah, I can on - ly i - mag -
Emaj7 E Emaj7 E
- ine. I can on - ly i - mag -

Asus2
Bsus
C♯m9
- ine, I can on-ly i-mag - ine.
Amaj7
I can on - ly i - mag - ine when all I
mp
B(add4)
G♯m/C♯
4fr
C♯m
4fr
E
will do is for-ev - er, for - ev - er wor - ship You.
Amaj9
B
E
I can on - ly i - mag - ine.

GOD OF WONDERS

Words and Music by MARC BYRD
and STEVE HINDALONG

Dsus
Em
Csus2
3fr
glo - ry to the Lord on high.
I will call Your name by night.
G
D
God of won - ders be - yond our gal - ax - y, You are
Am7
Csus2
3fr
ho - ly, ho - ly. The
G
D
u - ni - verse de - clares Your maj - es - ty. You are

Am7
Csus2
3fr
ho - ly,
ho - ly;
Lord of heav - en and earth,
1
Dsus
Em
Lord of heav-en and earth.
Csus2
3fr
Dsus
Em
Csus2
3fr

2
Am7
Hal - le - lu - jah to the
C
Lord of heav - en and earth.
Am7
Hal - le - lu - jah to the
C
Lord of heav - en and earth.
Am7
Hal - le - lu - jah to the
C
Lord of heav - en and earth.
G

INDESCRIBABLE

Words and Music by LAURA STORY
and JESSE REEVES

* *Recorded a half step higher.*

Gm
F/A
From the col - ors of Fall to the fra - grance of
Who i - mag - ined the sun and gives source to its
B♭
Cm
3fr
Spring,
light,
ev - 'ry crea - ture u -
yet con - ceals it to
B♭
A♭
4fr
E♭/G
3fr
F/A
nique in the song that it sings,
bring us the cool - ness of night?
all ex - claim - ing:
None can fath - om.
B♭
F
E♭
3fr
In - de - scrib - a - ble, un - con - tain - a - ble; You placed the stars in the

Gm
B♭/D
sky and You know them by name.
You are a - maz - ing,
E♭
B♭
God.
All pow - er - ful,
F
E♭
un - tam - a - ble;
awe - struck, we fall to our knees as we hum - bly pro -
Gm
B♭/D
E♭
- claim:
You are a - maz - ing,
God.

1
E♭maj7
3fr
2
Cm
3fr
B♭
You are a - maz - ing, __
A♭
4fr
__ God. ____
D♭
D♭/C♭

B♭
F
E♭
3fr
In - de - scrib - a - ble,
un - con - tain - a - ble;
You placed the stars in the
Gm
B♭/D
sky and You know them by
name.
You are a - maz - ing,
E♭
3fr
B♭
God.
All pow - er - ful,
In - com - p'ra - ble,
F
E♭
3fr
un - tam - a - ble;
awe - struck, we fall to our
knees as we hum - bly pro -
un - change - a - ble;
You see the depths of my
heart and You love me the

Gm
B♭/D
E♭
- claim:
same;
You are a - maz - ing,
God.
1
2
E♭maj7
You are a - maz - ing,
God.
rit.

JESUS FREAK

Words and Music by TOBY McKEEHAN
and MARK HEIMERMANN

F5
Ab5
4 fr
Eb5
Bb
C5
3 fr
ho.
Ha, ha.
F5
Ab5
4 fr
Eb5
Bb
C5
3 fr
Fm
Db5
4 fr
Bb
Sep - a - rat - ed, I cut my - self clean from a
Ka - mi - ka - ze, my death is gain. I've been
Fm
Db5
4 fr
Bb
past that comes back in my dark - est of dreams.
marked by my Mak - er a pe - cu - liar dis - play.

Fm
Db5
Bb
Been ap - pre - hend - ed by a spir - i - tual force and the
The high and loft - y, they see me as weak 'cause I
Fm
Db5
Bb
grace that re - placed all the me I've di - vorced. I saw a
won't live and die for the pow - er they seek, yeah. There was a
Fm
Db5
Bb5
man with a tat on his big fat bel - ly. It wig - gled a - round like mar - ma - lade jel - ly. It
man from the des - ert with naps in his head. The sand that he walked was al - so his bed. The
Fm
Db5
Bb5
took me a while to catch what it said 'cause I had to match the rhy - thm of his bel - ly with my head.
words that he spoke made the peo - ple as - sume there was - n't too much left in the up - per room. With
4 fr

Fm
Db5
4 fr
Bb5
"Je-sus saves"__ is what it raved_ in a typ - i - cal tat - too green. He
skins on his back and hair on his face, they thought he was strange_ by the lo-custs he ate._ You see, the
Fm
Db5
4 fr
Bb5
stood on a box in the mid-dle of the cit - y and he claimed he had__ a dream.__
Phar - i - sees tripped when they heard him_ speak_ un - til the king took the head of this Je - sus freak.
F5
Ab5
4 fr
Eb5
Bb5
C5
3 fr
What will peo - ple think__ when they hear that I'm__ a Je - sus freak?
F5
Ab5
4 fr
Eb5
Bb5
C5
3 fr
What will peo - ple do____ when they find that it's true?___

F5
Ab5
4 fr
Eb5
Bb5
C5
3 fr
I don't real - ly care ___ if they la - bel me a Je - sus freak.
F5
Ab5
4 fr
Eb5
Bb5
C5
3 fr
There ain't no dis - guis - ing the truth. ___
1
F5
There ain't no dis - guis - ing the truth, ___ though I ain't in - to hid - ing ___
___ the truth._
2, 3
F5
Ab5
4 fr
Eb5
Bb5
C5
3 fr
What will peo - ple think_ when they hear that I'm_ a Je - sus freak?

F5 Ab5 Eb5 Bb5 C5
4 fr
3 fr
What will peo - ple do when they find that it's true?
F5 Ab5 Eb5 Bb5 C5
I don't real - ly care if they la - bel me a Je - sus freak.
To Coda
F5 Ab5 Eb5 Bb5 C5
There ain't no dis - guis - ing the truth. No,
F5 Ab5 Eb5 Bb C5
I ain't in - to hid - ing.

F5
B♭/F
D♭/F
F5
B♭/F
D♭/F
F5
B♭/F
D♭/F
F5
People say I'm strange, does it make me a stranger that my best friend was born
1
B♭/F
D♭/F
in a manger?
2
B♭/F
D♭/F
N.C.
in a manger?
N.C.

1
2
D.S. al Coda
(take 2nd ending)
CODA
Bb5 C5 F5 Ab5 Eb5 Bb C5
What will peo-ple think?
(What will peo - ple think?)
F5 Ab5 Eb5 Bb5 C5 F5 Ab5 Eb5
What will peo-ple do?
(What will peo - ple do?)
I don't real-ly care.
Bb C5 F5 Ab5 Eb5 Bb5 C5 Fm
There ain't no dis-guis-ing the truth.
(What else can I say?)
(Je - sus is the way.)

SHINE

Words and Music by PETER FURLER
and STEVE TAYLOR

Em7
Am
that might per - suade a strict dic - ta - tor to re - tire, fire the ar -
- ma, it sure ain't fate that-'d make a Dead - head sell his van, that-'d make a schiz -
C/G
F
- my, teach the poor o - ri - ga - mi. The truth is in, the proof is when you hear your heart
- o - phren - ic turn in his cray - ons. O - prah freaks and sci - ence seeks a ra - tion - ale
G
C
start ask - ing, "What's my mo - ti - va - tion?"
that shall ex - cuse this strange be - hav - ior.
F
and try as you may, there is - n't a way to ex - plain
When you let it shine you will in - spire the kind of en -

Em7
Am
the kind of change that-'d make an Es - ki - mo re-nounce fur, that-'d make a veg -
- tire turn-a-round that-'d make a bounc - er take bal-let, e-ven bounc -
Am/G
F
- e - tar - i - an bar - be-cue ham - ster, un-less you can trace this a-bout - face
- ers who aren't... hap - py. But out of the glare with no-where to turn, you ain't gon-na learn
G
C
to a cer - tain sign.
it on "What's My Line?"
Shine. Make 'em won - der what you've got.
F/C
C
F5
Make 'em wish that they were not on the out - side look - in' bored.

C
F/C
Shine. Let it shine be - fore all men.
Let 'em see good works and then
C
F5
let 'em glo - ri - fy the Lord.
F
F/E
Dm7
(Shine, shine, shine, shine.) (Shine, shine,
F/C
F
F/E
shine, shine.) (Shine, shine, shine, shine.)

Dm7
F
G
C
Shine. Make 'em won - der what you've got.
F/C
C
F5
Make 'em wish that they were not on the out - side look - in' bored.
C
F/C
Shine. Let it shine be - fore all men. Let 'em see good works and then
C
1
F5
C
let 'em glo - ri - fy the Lord. Shine. Make 'em won - der what you've got.

F/C
C
Make 'em wish that they were not ___ on the out - side look - in' bored. ___
F5
C
___ Shine. Let it shine be - fore all men. ___
F/C
C
___ Let 'em see good works and then ___ let 'em glo - ri - fy the Lord. ___
F5
B♭sus2
2
F5
N.C.
___ ___ Shine.

STEP BY STEP

Words and Music by
DAVID STRASSER "BEAKER"

Am C/D G D/F♯ D C/E D
ways. And step by step You'll lead me, and I will fol-low You all of my
1 G C/E D
days. O
2 G Em
days. And I will fol-low You all of my
Dsus D C F C/D
days, and I will fol - low You all of my days. And
G/D D C/E D G
step by step You'll lead me, and I will fol-low You all of my days.
rit.

TESTIFY TO LOVE

Words and Music by PAUL FIELD, HENK POOL,
RALPH VAN MANEN and ROBERT RIEKERK

Cm
3 fr
A♭
4 fr
all the voic - es of ___ the wind,
from the riv - ers to ___ the sea,
E♭/G
3 fr
B♭sus
B♭
ev - 'ry dream that reach - es out, ___ that
ev - 'ry hand that reach - es out, ___ ev - 'ry
Cm
3 fr
A♭
4 fr
reach - es out ___ to find ___ where love ___ be - gins, ___
hand that reach - es out ___ to of - fer peace, ___
A♭
4 fr
Cm
3 fr
B♭sus
ev - 'ry word ___ of ev - 'ry sto - ry, ___
ev - 'ry sim - ple act ___ of mer - cy, ___

Cm
Bb
Ab
ev - 'ry star in ev - 'ry sky,
ev - 'ry step to king - dom come,
(Harmony 2nd time)
Fm7
Eb/G
Ab
Bb7sus
Bb7
Bb7sus
ev - 'ry cor - ner of cre - a - tion lives to tes - ti -
all the hope in ev - 'ry heart will speak what love has
Ab/Eb
Eb
fy.
done.
For as long as I shall
Bb
Cm
Cm/Bb
live, I will tes - ti - fy to love. I'll be a wit - ness in the si -

A♭
A♭/B♭
E♭
-lenc-es when words are not e-nough. With ev-'ry breath I
B♭
Cm
B♭
take, I will give thanks to God a-bove, for as long as I shall
1
A♭
E♭/B♭
B♭
E♭
live, I will tes-ti-fy to love.
2
A♭
E♭/B♭
B♭
E♭
live, I will tes-ti-fy to love.
Tes-ti-fy, tes-ti-fy.
Col-ors of the rain-bow, voic-es of the wind,

G♭
D♭/F
C♭maj7
Tes - ti - fy, tes - ti - fy.
dream that reach-es out where love be - gins,
word of ev - 'ry sto - ry, star in ev - 'ry sky,
1 B♭m7
D♭
E♭7
Tes - ti - fy, tes - ti - fy.
cor - ner of cre - a - tion tes - ti - fy.
Moun-tains to the val - leys, riv - ers to the sea,
G♭
C♭maj7
Tes - ti - fy, tes - ti - fy.
hand that reach-es out to of - fer peace, a
sim - ple act of mer - cy, king - dom come,
B♭m7
D♭
2 B♭m7
D♭
ev - 'ry heart will speak what love has done.
cor - ner of cre - a - tion tes - ti - fy.

E♭
B♭
For as long as I shall live, I'll
For as long as I shall live, I will tes - ti - fy to love.
Cm
Cm/B♭
A♭
A♭/B♭
tes - ti - fy, tes - ti - fy. All my life, I'll tes - ti - fy.
I'll be a wit - ness in the si - lenc - es when words are not e - nough.
E♭
B♭
Ev - 'ry breath I take, give thanks and
With ev - 'ry breath I take, I will give thanks to God a - bove,

Cm
B♭
A♭
A♭/B♭
B♭
tes - ti - fy, tes - ti - fy.
for as long as I shall live, I will tes - ti - fy.
F
C
2nd time:
For as long as I shall live, I'll
1st time: Parts
2nd time: Solo
For as long as I shall live, I will tes - ti - fy to love.
Dm
Dm/C
B♭
B♭/C
Am/C
tes - ti - fy, tes - ti - fy. All my life, I'll tes - ti - fy.
I'll be a wit - ness in the si - lenc - es when words are not e - nough.

F
C
For as long as I shall live, I'll
With ev - 'ry breath I take, I will give thanks to God a - bove,
Dm
C
1
B♭
F/C
C
tes - ti - fy, tes - ti - fy.
for as long as I shall live, I will tes - ti - fy to love.
2
B♭
F/C
C
F
All my life, I'll tes - ti - fy. Ev - 'ry breath I
live, I will tes - ti - fy to love.
Tes - ti - fy Your way,

C
Dm7
take, give thanks and tes - ti - fy, tes - ti - fy. All
tes - ti - fy Your truth, tes - ti - fy Your life, Your
B♭
Dm/C
C
F
C
my life, I'll tes - ti - fy. For as long as I shall live, I'll
love and mer - cy. Tes - ti - fy Your way, tes - ti - fy Your truth,
Dm7
B♭
Dm/C
C
F5
tes - ti - fy, tes - ti - fy. All my life, I'll tes - ti - fy.
tes - ti - fy Your life, Your love and mer - cy.

THY WORD

Words and Music by MICHAEL W. SMITH
and AMY GRANT

Ab/C
Bb/D
Eb
3fr
light unto my path.
Now
Bb/D
Fm
Cm
Gm
When I feel afraid, think I've lost my way,
I will not forget Your love for me and yet my
Ab
Bb
Ab/Eb
Eb
4fr
still You're there right beside me. And
heart forever is wandering.
Bb/D
Fm
Cm
Gm
nothing will I fear as long as You are near.
Jesus, be my guide and hold me to Your side, and

A♭
B♭
Csus(add2)
C
G/B
B♭sus2
A♭/B♭
4fr
Please be near me to the end.
I will love You to the end.
E♭
3fr
B♭/D
E♭
A♭/C
B♭/D
E♭
B♭/D
E♭
A♭/C
B♭/D
E♭

B♭/D
Fm
Cm
Gm
Noth - ing will I fear as long as You are near.
A♭
B♭
Csus(add2)
C
Please be near me to the end.
E♭
B♭/D
E♭
3fr
4fr
Thy Word is a lamp un - to my feet and a
A♭/C
B♭/D
1
E♭
light un - to my path.

2
E♭sus
6fr
E♭
3fr
A♭/C
3fr
B♭/D
path, and a light un - to my
E♭sus
6fr
E♭
3fr
A♭/C
3fr
B♭/D
path. You're the light un - to my
E♭5
6fr
E♭sus2
6fr
path.
8va
rit.

YOU PUT THIS LOVE IN MY HEART

Words and Music by
KEITH GREEN

Am
C
Am
I tried but could not re - fuse,
There are some times when I doubt,
Is all this real or a dream?
F
C/G
G
C
You gave me no time to choose,
You put this love in my heart.
but You al - ways find me out,
You put this love in my heart.
I feel so glad I could scream,
You put this love in my heart.
Am
G
F
C/E
Dm
G
(1., 3.) I wan - na know where the bad feel - in's go,
(2.) 'Cause when I've seen all that You've done for me,

F C/E Dm G G♯dim7
when I'm de - pressed and I get down so low, and
it's hard to doubt I just have to be - lieve, 'cause You
Am C D Am C D
then I see You com - in' to me and it's al -
fol - low up prov - in' all of Your love.
To Coda
1
F G F/G Em/G Dm/G
- right.
gliss.
2
F/G Em/G Dm/G F/C C
Well, I know the
gone now I'll

B♭
F
Dm7
F/G
lone - li - ness I had be - fore,
nev - er feel it an - y - more.
is
'Cause your
G/A
Dmaj9
G/A
lov - in' has re - leased me from all that's in my past
Dmaj7
B♭/C
Fmaj9
and I know I can be - lieve You, yeh, when You say
B♭/C
B♭maj7
Gm7
I'll nev - er be for - sak - en, Your love is gon - na last.

G9sus
3fr
G
G9sus
3fr
G
N.C.
D.C. al Coda
CODA
F/G
Em/G
Dm/G
F
C/G
G
You put this love in my heart,
gliss
F
C/G
G
F
C/G
G
You put this love in my heart, You put this love in my heart.
C
Am
F
C/G
G
C/G
Repeat and Fade
(You put this love in my heart) Woo, woo, woo, You put this love in my heart.